WELSH
NARROW GAUGE
ALBUM

P. B. WHITEHOUSE   OBE , ARPS

in association with

JOHN ADAMS   FIBP, ARPS

LONDON

IAN ALLAN

SBN 7110 0081 6

PRINTED BY IAN ALLAN (PRINTING) LTD SHEPPERTON MIDDLESEX

WELSH NARROW GAUGE

ALBUM

16/=

Contents

Preface

Few visitors to North Wales these days have not heard of the narrow gauge lines emanating from Portmadoc, Towyn or Aberystwyth. Fewer still are unaware of Snowdon's steam operated rack railway—the easy but expensive way to reach the summit. But there was a time not so long ago, when the future of the little railways of Wales seemed far from secure, for the flow of continuous freight traffic which was their original raison d'etre had been crumbling away for decades. The fact that the lines are operating today, purely as tourist attractions, is due to one thing only—that a sufficient number of people want them to. These people can be divided into two quite separate categories—the enthusiast and the general public. The enthusiast provides the vital germ which ensures restoration and preservation, whilst the general public provides the support in passengers which is money. Both ingredients are vital if life is to be prolonged on any such enterprise. But it must always be remembered that without the public there can be no railway and the purist preservationist has to give way to reality, which means an efficient service mixed with an adequate degree of comfort. That this is happening is a feather in the cap of all those who have sought to keep the plumes of steam surging high on the narrow gauge railways of Wales. Long may it continue.

This book is intended as a pictorial record of the Welsh tourist lines as they are today and a reminder to both those who work and travel on them of happy days of steam in the valleys. There is a peculiar thrill in riding behind *"Merddin Emrys"* or *"Sir Haydn"* or perhaps B.R's *"Owain Glendower"* and listening to the sound of their exhausts reverberating among the hills proclaiming that they are still alive and very much kicking. A new generation is also rising, one which has probably never ridden on a main line train, this too finds the narrow gauge rewarding and fascinating.

In the historical introduction I have tried to provide a potted history of the rise, fall, and rebirth of the Welsh narrow gauge for pictures are of little interest without their why and wherefore. For the text I have modified parts of the introduction to my earlier *"Narrow Gauge Album"* now out of print and I hope that this precis will be of interest to those who visit the lines concerned and want to know just that little bit more.

P.B.W.

Tan-y-bwlch station on the Festiniog Railway early in the century. *[Festiniog Railway Co.*

▲ A Corris Railway passenger train crosses the river Dovey behind one of the three Falcon-built 0–4–2 tanks.
[*Author's Collection*

▼ On the Welsh Highland Railway, No. 11 *Moel Tryfan,* Fairlie 0–6–4 T on train from Portmadoc at Dinas Junction in June 1925.

Introduction

There is very little doubt that the Principality of Wales was father to the narrow gauge railway as we have known it in our life-time. The cradle was almost certainly the mountains and slate quarries of the North, and the Penrhyn Railway running north westwards from that quarry to Port Penrhyn on the Menai Straight the eldest child. This line like most of its brethren performed the marriage between the source of material so necessary to the Industrial Revolution and water-borne transport.

Steam, on the narrow gauge, came to Wales in January 1863. This was on the Festiniog Railway which had been open for traffic since 1836 and was prospering considerably—horses no longer being able to cope with the volume of slate on offer from the quarries at Blaenau Festiniog. History was made in 1865 when, after an inspection by Captain Tyler of the Board of Trade, the line was thrown open to public passengers. The Festiniog's steam locomotives were followed almost at once by two machines on the newly opened Talyllyn Railway which began to carry passengers from Towyn to Abergynolwyn in 1866.

Welshpool and Llanfair—*The Earl* waits with a mixed train at Llanfair Caereinion in 1925. Note the coach painted in GWR livery.   [*Author's Collection*

▲ *Sir Theodore* of the Glyn Valley Tramway.

[*Author's Collection*

▶ One of the Vale of Rheidol, Swindon-built 2–6–2 tank locomotives, No 8. at Swindon Works in the early thirties. [*S. J. Rhodes*

▼ A Talyllyn Railway train behind the ancient 0–4–2 well tank *Dolgoch* at Dolgoch [*Author's Collection*

These two projects proved so successful that other railways were promoted and built for the same purposes with locomotive traction—for example, the Festiniog & Blaenau, and the North Wales Narrow Gauge, both to the Festiniog's gauge of 2' 0" nominal, and the Corris, Machynlleth & River Dovey Tramroad, to the Talyllyn's 2' 3". On the latter the traffic was still horse drawn until 1879, when the title of the line was altered to the Corris Railway.

By the mid-1870's steam-worked narrow gauge railways had begun in the Isle of Man and also in Ireland, their promotion being largely due to the Festiniog's happy example, and to the heavy propaganda put out by its engineer Charles Spooner. It is interesting to speculate on the possibilities which existed for narrow gauge rails at the time, for not only was Spooner considering a 2' 0" gauge project which could have led to a network of lines throughout Snowdonia, but the great "Premier Line" —the London & North Western Railway, had it in mind to extend its existing standard gauge branch, then terminating at Betwsycoed by the narrow gauge to join the Festiniog's at Blaenau. But in the event it was only the North Wales Narrow Gauge which came into being, passenger trains running from Dinas, near Caernarvon to South Snowdon by 1881. This was not a very happy railway being conceived without a foundation of continuous goods traffic, and it failed to carry out its programme which was more extensive than is generally known—it fell into the hands of a receiver within a few years.

Once established for the carriage of freight the little lines began to carry passengers casually. Usually this started by the occasional local resident taking an unofficial lift and this in time snowballed until public demand justified the provision of a special wagon or coach. So each in its own individual way, the Welsh Railways consolidated themselves; for the most part they ran close to seaside tourist areas now becoming popular with holiday makers from the Midlands and North West, and the miners or villagers trains became more heavily loaded in the summer weeks. Thus as well as serving the lonely outposts the railways also provided a means of relaxation to the slowly growing number of visitors to the Welsh coast. Such lines as the Glyn Valley Tramway (Based on Chirk, close to the Welsh-English border) were more on the English pattern of rural branches or tramways and carried less tourist traffic.

The 1890's produced the next batch of Welsh openings, largely due to the Light Railways Act introduced in 1896. One exception was the Snowdon Mountain Railway, the only steam rack-operated line in the British Isles. This was an extremely notable achievement when one considers that the work was completed in fourteen months—December 1894 to January 1896— construction being carried out entirely by hand. The benign influence of the Light Railway Act encouraged the

construction of the 2′ 0″ guage Vale of Rheidol in 1902 and the 2′ 6″ gauge Welshpool and Llanfair Light Railway in 1903. Both these lines were worked by the Cambrian Railway—although the Rheidol was independant for its first nine years. Neither were in the old tradition of slate carriers, being passenger and mainly rural lines respectively. (The Rheidol's freight was mainly based on lead ore from some short lived mines). The next decade saw the introduction of better roads, the car and the early omnibus, and it was the beginning of the decline.

During the 1914–18 war, traffic nearly ceased on the North Wales Narrow Gauge but with hope born in the rosy hues of Peace a new future was predicted for it. The line was thoroughly relaid throughout its length and extended by 1923 to join the former Croesor Tramway, which in its turn was relaid to passenger train standards. A short section of track between this and the Festiniog at Portmadoc was constructed and the biggest white elephant of the British narrow gauge came into being. The new railway was given the title of "Welsh Highland" and this, together with the Festiniog (now a light railway) fell into the hands of the North Wales Power and Traction Company who appointed the redoubtable Colonel H. F. Stephens as Engineer to both Companies, putting Spooners Empire under the Colonel's jurisdiction and adding them to his already extensive menagerie of small railways. So it was that the first trains over the new line were hauled by two of the pioneer steam locomotives on the narrow gauge—the Festiniog's *Prince* and *Princess.*

The inter-war years saw a steep decline in the fortunes of the narrow gauge lines, but strangely enough they also provided the foundations of the revival, now so evident—tourist traffic. Slowly but surely the need for slate had been disappearing, no longer was it required to roof the houses of the growing cities—machine made tiles were cheaper. This trend had started in the Edwardian era but the price of labour and transport made sure of it by the early 1930's and as the North Wales Narrow Gauge found out some fifty years before, continuous flows of freight are the life blood of any railway either narrow or standard gauge. The tourists helped, but that was all. By the outbreak of the Second World War in 1939 the only narrow gauge lines still operating a passenger service were those in the mountains of Wales. The Festiniog was open, as was the Talyllyn, and the former Vale of Rheidol now owned by the Great Western Railway. The Corris carried freight on a shoe-string and the Welshpool line still eked out a living among the Montgomery farmers. It was getting thin. The War 1939–45 put an end to the passenger services on all but the ageing and somewhat decrepit Talyllyn, which carried on protected by the dogged-ness of its venerable owner and Manager, Sir Henry Haydn Jones who vowed that so long as he lived, the railway would run. This promise was kept.

Throughout the war the Festiniog still ran a goods service from Blaenau down to the exchange sidings at Minfford but the line beyond Boston Lodge and across the Cob to the Harbour was little used. The Corris also continued to bring the odd load of slate down from Aberllefenni to Machynlleth, and the W. & L. was really doing quite well. The disastrous Welsh Highland had gone in 1937 almost dragging its partner the Festiniog with it and this line only barely survived hostilities; on August 1st 1946 the staff were given notice, and the line closed, and soon took on an air of desolation and decay.

But it was the Great Western Railway and Sir Haydn Jones who saved the day. Swindon being somehow more autocratic yet more human and adventurous than the others making up the Big Four, took the advice of its Divisional Officer and had a go—the Rheidol re-opened for the summer service in 1945. The Talyllyn was still creeping on and the last slate was being hacked from the dangerous galleries at Abergynolwyn, Sir Haydn still lived, but it was not to be for long. In 1948 serious flooding of the River Dovey snapped the life's thread of the Corris and it gave up the ghost.

A wartime picture of the Talyllyn Railway taken at Dolgoch. The engine is *Talyllyn*. [*W. A. Camwell*

In the summer of 1950 Sir Haydn Jones died. To those who knew and loved the little lines of Wales this seemed to be the end, but in truth it was a new beginning.

In October of that year a great doyen of lost causes, author L.T.C. Rolt, himself an engineer of no mean standing, along with two of his friends W.G. Trinder and Jim Russell, called a meeting in Birmingham to see what could be done to save the Talyllyn which was, by then, the oldest surviving steam-hauled narrow gauge line in the world. The outcome of that meeting and the formation of the Talyllyn Railway Preservation Society is too well known to be recorded here in detail, but it must be said that any success here is due to the generosity of Lady Haydn Jones who readily agreed to the shares of the company being handed over to a Holding Company controlled by the new Preservation Society.

Nothing succeeds like success, and inspired by the new life on the Talyllyn, others, led by Alan Pegler of *Flying Scotsman* fame, got down to brass tacks with the Festiniog which re-opened in part in the summer of 1955. This was followed in 1963 by the Welshpool and Llanfair Light Railway Company (a Society limited by guarantee) who leased the line and acquired the stock after the line had closed in 1956.

So the years since 1950 have been exciting ones where achievements have taken place which many considered impossible. Near derelict lines have been restored to healthy life and in all cases improved beyond their progenitors wildest dreams. New locomotives and rolling stock have been built and permanent way preserved, new blood has fused with old and these now solely tourist lines are known throughout the world. Who would have thought that the Talyllyn's record number of passengers carried in the 1950 season (5,000) would have gone up over 20 times and that Festiniog could carry 300,000 passengers in one summer? It has been a task of devotion by professionals and amateurs who have become new professionals. Determination has made sure of success.

Penrhyn Quarry locomotive *Pamela* at the Quarry on shunting duty.

Berstein and *Maid Marion* back to back at Dinorwic.
[*Ivo Peters*]

On the Padarn Railway's main line (4 ft. gauge) showing how the 2 ft, gauge wagons were carried in "piggy-back" fashion.
[*Ivo Peters*]

But what of the others ? The pure slate lines have gone—there is no longer steam at Penrhyn or Padarn and the Corris is taken up and its engines work on the Talyllyn. The Snowdon continues to attract its crowds of tourists and it is hoped that the future here is secure. This leaves the British Rail owned Vale of Rheidol, a line which could be the finest of them all—where does its future lie ?

Twenty years ago, just after Nationalisation the Rheidol, apart from the Snowdon Mountain Railway, was the only respectable passenger carrying narrow gauge railway in Wales. Now, compared with the privately owned preserved and restored lines it has fallen sadly behind. This can scarely be held to be B.R.'s fault, for the circumstances are very different. Even the Talyllyn and Festiniog Railways are not really profitable; there is a small surplus from running the trains but money is also obtained from other sources unavailable to B.R. such as the railway shop and members subscriptions. This money can be spent on improvements and new equipment. B.R. cannot possibly work like this, it is a business and by Act of Parliament it is bound to spend money only when a proper economic return can be seen. At present the future is insecure, for each section of B.R. must either make a profit—which the Rheidol does not, or be subsidised. If the Government give it no subsidy it will be closed. Does its future too lie with private preservation ? This could be the answer.

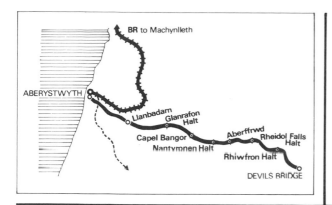

Vale of Rheidol Railway

Vale of Rheidol

Now British Railways only steam line the 2′ 0″ gauge line from Aberystwyth to Devil's Bridge is a must for both the tourist and railway enthusiast. Its coastal terminus is B.R's mainline station in the centre of Aberystwyth.

▼ No. 9 *Prince of Wales* approaching Devil's Bridge.
[*David Mitchell*

▲ No. 7 *Owain Glyndwr* in the shed at Aberystwyth.

▶ No. 9 *Prince of Wales* in the new platform at Aberystwyth
station on the opening day 1968.   [*David Mitchell*

▲ No. 9 *Prince of Wales* outside the shed at Aberyswyth.　　　　　　　　[*Ivo Peters*

No. 8 *Llywelyn* waiting on train in old station at Aberystwyth.

[*P. B. Whitehouse*

▲ No. 7 *Owain Glyndwr* crossing road after leaving
Aberystwyth Station.   [*P. B. Whitehouse*

◀ No. 9 *Prince of Wales*.
[*David Mitchell*

19

No. 7 *Owain Glyndwr* heading for Devil's Bridge near Capel Bangor.
[*A. Robey*

No 7 *Owain Glyndwr* near Capel Bangor.
[*D. J. Brown*

▲ No. 9 *Prince of Wales* takes water at Aberffrwd.
[*Ivo Peters*

▼ No. 9 *Prince of Wales* arriving at Aberffrwd.
[*David Mitchell*

No. 7 *Owain Glyndwr* starting away from Aberffrwd.

No. 9 *Prince of Wales* and train in the woods near
Rheidol Falls Halt. [*A. Robey*

▲ No. 9 *Prince of Wales* round the 'S' curve near Devil's Bridge.
[*David Mitchell*

▼ No. 9 *Prince of Wales* approaching Devil's Bridge.
[*David Mitchell*

▲ No. 8 *Llewelyn* ready to leave Devil's Bridge for Aberystwyth.

[*P. B. Whitehouse*

25

Heading up the valley.

[C. C Green

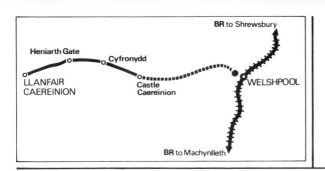

Welshpool & Llanfair Railway

Welshpool & Llanfair

The only narrow gauge railway to have no coastal terminus this 2′6″ gauge line is cut off from its former terminal point at Welshpool and operates from a headquarters at Llanfair Caereinion. It has the advantage of being relatively close to the Midlands and can be visited from them in a day quite easily. The W. & L. is essentially a line run by the new professionals; amateurs who give their time to run trains and maintain the track which is leased from British Railways. The Company welcomes visitors and like its sisters further west is keen to have new helpers. Details are available from the Welshpool & Llanfair Light Railway Ltd., Llanfair Caereinion, Montgomeryshire.

▼ No. 822 in B.R. days waiting to leave Welshpool with an enthusiasts' special. [*Ivo Peters*

◀ No. 822 with a freight bound for Welshpool station is held up at Seven Stars whilst a car is pushed out of the way. *[P. B. Whitehouse*

▲ No. 822 leaves Seven Stars in Welshpool with a local train for Llanfair in 1956. *[P. B. Whitehouse*

◀ No. 822 shunts in Welshpool Market in B.R. days. *[P. B. Whitehouse*

▲ No. 822 heads a Locomotive Club of Great Britain
special towards Llanfair.   [*Ivo Peters*

▲ No. 1 *The Earl* hauling the inaugural train, re-openin
the railway under the Preservation Society.
[P. B. Whitehou

▼ *The Earl* (formerly No. 822) now W & LR No. 1 pos
in a sylvan setting. *[Ivo Pet*

No. 822 with enthusiasts special heads away from Raven Square.

[*P. B. Whitehouse*

No. 822 returning to Welshpool with a train of empty wagons.
[*P. B. Whitehouse*

The morning goods returns through the woods.
[*P. B. Whitehouse*

No. 2 *Countess* leaves the water stop near Llanfair Caereinion.
[*E. J. Dew*

▲ No. 1 *The Earl* with a ballast train at Castle Caereinion
station.   [*P. B. Whitehouse*

▼ In the floods of 1965 the bridge over the River Banwy
was damaged and things looked black.   [*F. J. Hastilow*

▲ Valiant work by members and the Royal Engineers rebuilt the bridge.   [*F. J. Hastilow*]

▼ The first passenger train crosses the bridge after rebuilding (August 1965).   [*F. J Hastilow*]

▲ No. 1 *The Earl* with ballast train on viaduct between
Castle Caereinion and Llanfair Caereinion.

[*P. B. Whitehouse*

▲ No. 1 *The Earl* runs parallel with the River Banwy near
Llanfair Caereinion in 1968.   [*Allan Stewart*

▲ No. 1 *The Earl* poses in the sidings at Castle Caereinion
station.   [*P. B. Whitehouse*

One of the Zillertalbahn coaches arriving at Welshpool station for trans-shipment to the Welshpool & Llanfair Railway.   [*F. J. Hastilow*

Monarch—a glimpse of the future?   [*P. B. Whitehouse*

▲ *Countess* climbs the bank beyond Raven Square with
the daily goods.
                                                  [P. B. Whitehouse

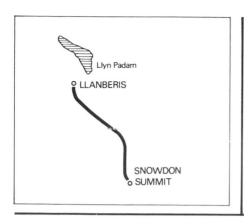

Snowdon Mountain Railway

Snowdon

This is Britain's only steam operated rack railway and is now one of the few left in Europe. Based on the village of Llanberis, close to Llyn Padarn the line clings to the face of the highest mountain in Wales.

▼ Snowdon Mountain Railway Motive Power Depot at Llanberis with locomotive Nos. 6 and 7.   [*John H. Bird*

▲ No. 7 crossing the viaduct with a down train on the
approach to Llanberis. [*V. C K. Allen*

▶ No. 5 with up train crossing viaduct after leaving
Llanberis. [*I. S. Pearsall*

44

No. 7 Departs from Halfway station with an up train.
[John H. Bird

No. 4 with an up train between Halfway and Clogwyn.
[*John H. Bird*

No. 6 ascending with up train with a backdrop of Moel Eillo.

[*John H. Bird*

▲ No. 2 waits at Clogwyn Station.   [R. E. Vincent

The last lap approaching summit.
[*M. Dunnett*

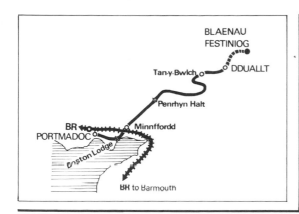

Festiniog Railway

Festiniog

The Festiniog Railway, built to Spooner's gauge of a nominal 2' 0" is perhaps the best known of all sub standard gauge lines, in fact so famous did it become during its early years that it set the pattern of railway construction in many countries overseas. Like its smaller sister the Talyllyn, the Festiniog has its westerly terminus on the shores of the Irish Sea, this time in Caernarvonshire at Portmadoc. The whole of the line has not yet been re-opened but trains now run beyond Tanybwlch to Ddault. The organisation here is a little more formal than on the Talyllyn but there is a supporters side in the Festiniog Railway Society whose members are encouraged to work on the railway in their spare time. Details can be obtained from the Festiniog Railway, Harbour Station, Portmadoc, Caernarvonshire.

▼ *Prince* approaching Boston Lodge in the early days of the renewed Festiniog.   [*P. B. Whitehouse*

▲ *Taliesin* now renamed *Earl of Merioneth* leaves Portmadoc Harbour station with a train of modern bogie stock in the rear. [*P. B. Whitehouse*

To overcome a severe locomotive shortage the FR purchased two of the Penrhyn Quarry Railway's ex "main line" locomotives—*Linda* and *Blanche. Linda*
▼ is seen here at Portmadoc Harbour station. [*P. B. Whitehouse*

'The Water Hole'— a firemans-eye view of *Prince* having refreshment. This locomotive built in 1865 was one of the first steam engines to run on the narrow gauge.

[*Stephen Evans*

A portrait of *Prince* on the Cob at Boston Lodge. The driver is Bill Hoole of LNER and, (Eastern Region), fame. He came to the FR after his retirement and *Prince* became his regular engine.

[*P. B. Whitehouse*

▲ Early days at Boston Lodge.
[*Leicester Mercury*

◄ A gull's-eye view of *Linda* approaching Boston Lodge from the Cob. Note the slotted signal and entrance tracks to the shed and works. [*David Mitchell*

▼ *Taliesin (Earl of Merioneth)* poses for a picture on the Cob just outside Boston Lodge shed. [*P. B. Whitehouse*

The old disc signal between Boston Lodge and Minffordd.
[*P. B. Whitehouse*

Earl of Merioneth accelerating past Boston Lodge Halt.
[*N. F. Gurley*

▲ An up ballast train hauled by *Earl of Merioneth* standing
in the passing loop at Minffordd.   [*N. F. Gurley*

▼ *Taliesin (Earl of Merioneth)* being admired by passengers
while standing at Minffordd.   [*N. F. Gurley*

Prince with an up train leaves Penrhyn. [*Festiniog Railway Co.*

The double Fairlie *Taliesin (Earl of Merioneth)* whistles for the road crossing at Penrhyn. [*Derek Cross*

◀ *Taliesin (Earl of Merioneth)*
with train on Gwyndy Bank.
Bill Hoole on the footplate.
[*G. Roscoe*

▼ Alco-Cooke 2–6–2 tank
at Whistling Curve on the
last train of 1968.
[*N. F. Gurley*

◀ *Earl of Merioneth* heading through Gysgfa.
[*Daniel H. Wilson*

▶ Back and front at Tan-y-bwlch *Prince* and *Taliesin (Earl of Merioneth).*
[*N. F. Gurley*

▼ "Centenary" Special 1963 at Tan-y-bwlch. This picture was taken on the "Centenary" day with the then newly-out-of-shops *Merddin Emrys,* and guard in period costume.
[*P. B. Whitehouse*

◀ A Festiniog Day—24 hour train indicator at Tan-y-bwlch.
[John Adams

▶ *Prince* and Peasant—No. 0–6–0 diesel *Moelwyn* at Tan-y-bwlch.
[John Adams

▼ Isn't he lovely ?—*Prince* at Tan-y-bwlch.
[John Adams

▲ Sheep Pens—Crowd control equipment at Tan-y-bwlch.
[John Adams

WHEN THIS GATE IS CLOSED, KEEP TO
THE PLATFORM-TRAIN IS COMING!

▲ *Earl of Merioneth* with down train passing Dduallt
  P.W. hut.   [*N. F. Gurley*

▶ The first train to Dduallt April 6, 1968.

                                              [*R. G. Norris*

Earl of Merioneth heading for Dduallt. [*N. F. Gurley*

LIMITED CLEARANCE
DO NOT WALK
ALONG THE LINE

Pilot engine *Prince* at Dduallt Station with volunteers working on the loop.
[*Stephen Evans*

The Future lies ahead (1) Volunteers at work— deviationists extending their embankment (April 1968).
[*Stephen Evans*

The Future lies ahead (2) *Blanche* and ballast train at Dduallt Station.
[*Stephen Evans*

On Reflection

▲ "Fairlie's Ghost"—*Merddin Emrys* mirrored in a pool.
[*N. F. Gurley*

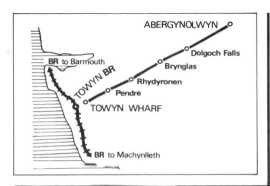

Talyllyn Railway

Talyllyn

This 2' 3" gauge railway in Merioneth, running from Towyn up the valley of the Afon Fathew to Abergynolwyn, was the first of all the narrow gauge railways to be preserved. It is now controlled by the Talyllyn Railway Preservation Society, many of whose members work voluntarily on the line during weekends and on their holidays. Full details of membership of the Society can be obtained from the Company's Office at Wharf Station, Towyn Merioneth.

▼ 1965 was the Talylyn's Centenary Year and that summer various special events marked this historic occasion, one of which was when the line was visited by the VSCC for a rally. Here a veteran Swift watches over the rebuilt No. 1 *Talyllyn.*

[*P. B. Whitehouse*

▶ No. 1 *Talyllyn* and No. 4 *Edward Thomas*—a typical morning scene at Pendre Yard. [*P. B. Whitehouse*

▲ No. 2 *Dolgoch* in Pendre Yard (West) after preliminary trials when returned to Towyn after rebuilding. This was a very complete job and little remains of the original engine. [*John Adams*

▶ No. 1 *Talyllyn* photographed while shunting at Pendre shortly after her rebuilding in 1964. Like her sister *Dolgoch* she is a renewal rather than a rebuild. [*P. B. Whitehouse*

▲ Pendre Workshops in 1968 with No. 3 *Sir Haydn* nearing completion after an extensive rebuild, a larger part of which was done by skilled volunteer labour.

[*David Mitchell*

▲ Three in a row at Pendre (Left to Right No. 2, No. 6 and No. 4)
[*David Mitchell*

▼ Chief Engineer John Bate and No. 6 *Douglas* in shops at Pendre.
[*P. B. Whitehouse*

▲ No. 2 *Dolgoch* with a down train leaving Rhydyronen.
[*John Adams*

◀ The ancient No. 2 *Dolgoch* at Rhydyronen in 1952 complete with rake of original TR stock, all built for the opening of the railway in 1865/6. [*Rimmer*

▼ No. 4 *Edward Thomas* approaching Rhydronen with an afternoon train.

No. 4 *Edward Thomas* with a down train passing No. 3 *Sir Haydn* at Brynglas just after the loop was built. This was the period when the upper stretch of the railway was being relaid by the Territorial Army.

[*P. B. Whitehouse*

No. 6 *Douglas* approaching Brynglas with an up afternoon train.

[*John Adams*

No. 4 *Edward Thomas* with an up afternoon train is called forward from the loop into Brynglas station.

[*P. B. Whitehouse*

No. 2 *Dolgoch* with the up morning train with refreshments van, heading up the valley east of Ryhdyronen.
[*John Adams*

▲ Volunteer working party ballasting on a bright spring afternoon between Brynglas and Dolgoch. [*John Adams*

◀ No. 6 *Douglas* waiting at Brynglas with an up train.
[*John Adams*

No. 2 *Dolgoch* takes water and is admired by passengers
at Dolgoch Falls Station. [*P. B. Whitehouse*

▲ The Old No. 2 *Dolgoch* crossing Dolgoch Viaduct in 1951 with the original T.R. Stock of 1865. [*John Adams*

▼ The new No. 1 *Talyllyn* crossing Dolgoch Viaduct in 1964. [*John Adams*

▲ No. 4 *Edward Thomas* leaving Dolgoch Falls with the up morning train
[*David Mitchell*

◀ No. 1 *Talyllyn* with up train east of Dolgoch Falls.
[*David Mitchell*

▶ No. 1 *Talyllyn* puts on a show at Dolgoch Falls.
[*John Adams*

▲ No. 6 *Douglas* pilots No. 4 *Edward Thomas* with an up morning train near Quarry Sidings.   [*David Mitchell*

◄ No. 4 *Edward Thomas* about to leave Dolgoch Falls with an up train on a spring morning in 1968.
[*C. M. Whitehouse*

▼ No. 2 *Dolgoch* with the up moring train photographed against a background of Mountain, east of Dolgoch Falls.
[*Rimmer*

▲ No. 3 *Sir Haydn* with a late afternoon train waiting to
leave Abergynolwyn.   [*P. B. Whitehouse*

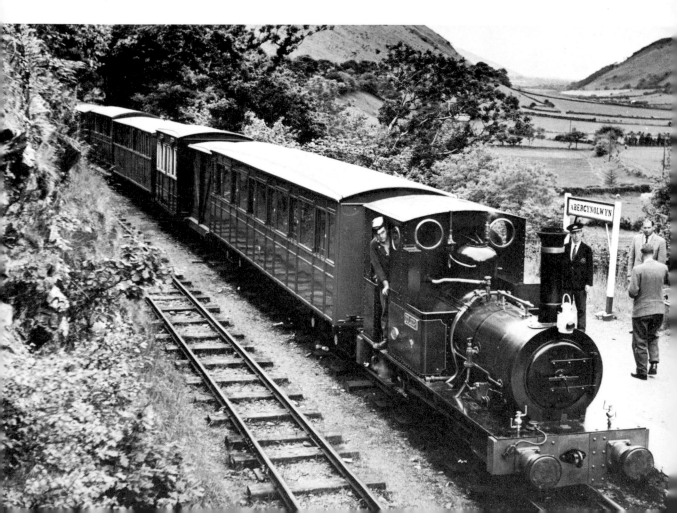

▲ No. 4 *Edward Thomas* at Abergynolwyn on a summer afternoon. *[John Adams*

◀ *Dolgoch* arrives at Abergynolwyn with the morning train. *[John Adams*

▼ No. 6 *Douglas* at Abergynolwyn. The late Earl of Northesk talks to a visitor. *[John Adams*

▲ Talyllyn in the 60s. The Gieslized No. 4 *Edward Thomas* pilots the rejuvenated No. 1 *Talyllyn* on a morning train from Wharf.

[*David Mitchell*

Beyond Abergynolwyn is the old mineral line which runs up the Nant Gwernol Ravine, to be opened one day as an extension—a bridge in need of repair. A hope for the future.

[*David Mitchell*